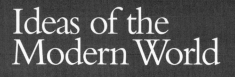

Ideas of the Modern World

Nationalism

Richard Tames

Raintree

Chicago, Illinois

**Library of Congress Cataloging-in-
Publication Data:**

Tames, Richard.
   Nationalism / Richard Tames.
      v. cm. -- (Ideas of the modern world)
Includes bibliographical references and index.
Contents: What is nationalism? -- The birth
of modern nationalism -- Nations and
empires -- Empires into nations --
Nationalism and communism -- Beyond the
nation-state -- Nationalism: today and
tomorrow.
   ISBN 0-7398-6417-3
   1. Nationalism--Juvenile literature. [1.
Nationalism.] I. Title. II.
Series.
   JC311.T2944 2003
   320.54--dc21

2003000913

Series design: Simon Borrough

1 2 3 4 5 6 7 8 9 0
LB 08 07 06 05 04

Printed in Hong Kong

Acknowledgments
The publisher would like to thank the
following for permission to reproduce
photographs:

pp. 4, 8, 14, 20, 26, 29, 32, 37, 41, 45, 48
Topham Picturepoint; pp. 7 (reused on
contents page), 51, 61 Rex; pp. 9, 10
(reused on p. 61), 12, 15, 17, 21, 23, 25,
31, 35, 38, 39, 44 Popperfoto;
pp. 13, 24, 27, 30 Mary Evans Picture
Library; p. 16 Hodder Wayland Picture
Library (Yale University Art Gallery);
p. 18 Peter Newark's American Pictures;
p.19 Corbis; p. 22 Peter Newark's
Military Pictures; p. 33 Camera Press;
p. 40 Peter Newark's Pictures; p. 43
Hodder Wayland Picture Library
(Illustrated London News);
p. 46 Hodder Wayland Picture Library;
pp. 47, 54–55, 58, 59
Popperfoto/Reuter; pp. 52, 56–57 and
title page (UNEP/Allen Tannenbaum).

Cover photo shows international flags
(Lester Lefkowitz/CORBIS)

Contents

What Is Nationalism?

Nationalism is the feeling that people in a country or area all belong together and are different from people in other places. The word nationalism comes from the word "nation." People often use the words "nation" or "state" to mean the same thing as "country." In some contexts, such as history and sociology, it is important to use these words more precisely.

Nations and states

A nation is a group of people whose members believe that the they share something (culture, genetics, language, religion, history, customs, or lifestyle) that binds them together in a way that makes them different and distinct from other groups of people. What defines a nation can be very controversial. A state is a **territory** controlled by a government. A state can be made up of more than one nation.

Nationalists believe that the peoples of the world are made up of distinct nations, each of which ought to have its own state. They think that ideally all states

A nation reborn—again. Demonstrators in Vilnius, the capital of Lithuania, demanding national independence in 1990. An empire five centuries ago, Lithuania was annexed by Russia in 1795, regained its independence in 1918, and was taken over again by the USSR in 1940. It became independent again in 1991.

should be **nation-states**, each made up of a single group of people. But for most of history, this has not been the case. The most powerful states have been empires or kingdoms, often made up of different groups of people. In empires loyalty was to a ruler, not to your fellow citizens.

Smaller states have often been based on a single city. For example, for a thousand years what we call Italy was divided into dozens of separate states. Italians thought of themselves not as Italians but as belonging to a city, such as Venice or Florence, or a region, like Tuscany or Sicily. The emergence of nationalism from the time of the French Revolution in 1789 (see page 19) persuaded Italians that, because they shared a common language and culture, they should unite together into a nation-state.

Defining nations

In 1861 the British philosopher John Stuart Mill (1806–1873) stated in his book *Representative Government*:

A portion of mankind may be said to constitute [make up] a nationality if they are united among themselves by common sympathies which do not exist between them and any others—which make them cooperate more willingly than with other people, desire to be under the same government, and desire that it should be government by themselves. . . .

What nationalists believe

Nationalism is based on the following set of beliefs:

1. The human race naturally is made up of nations.
2. Nations can be known by features that their members share, such as race, language, or religion.
3. The only rightful form of government is **self-determination**—the government of a nation by its own people. Each nation should have its own independent state, and the world should be made up of nation-states.

However, these beliefs are not as obviously true as nationalists have often thought. For example, religions have traditionally taught that being Christian, Hindi, Jewish, or Muslim was far more important than the country a person happened to be born in or the particular language that person spoke.

5

There has never been one agreed-on defintion of what the signs of **nationhood** are. Some think a nation is defined by a single language spoken by all its members and no one else, like Polish or Finnish. Others think it is possible for a nation to speak a language shared with others—like Arabic, English, or Spanish—and still be a separate nation by having a separate history or religion.

Unifying an existing nation into a single state is one way of creating a **nation-state**, as in the case of Italy or Germany in the 1800s. Another way is for an existing state to take on the character of a nation, as in the case of Japan (see page 31). Another way is for a nation to break away from an existing **multinational state**, like Greece (see page 22) or to throw off **colonial rule**, as in the case of Britain's thirteen **colonies** in North America (see page 16).

Throughout the 19th and 20th centuries, new nation–states came into being. After World War I (1914–1918), the League of Nations was set up to try to solve disputes between nations peacefully. It eventually had 63 states as members. The United Nations, set up as a successor to the League after World War II (1939–1945), now has three times as many members. This increase is largely because many former colonies of European states have become independent, and some multinational states, such as the former USSR and Yugoslavia, have split up.

Ideas and emotions

Nationalism is not just a set of ideas that appeal to people's reason. It is a powerful force that taps into people's feelings of pride, fear, and hatred. Nationalism is expressed through symbols such as flags, songs, poems, legends, and statues. It is an ever-changing set of ideas rather than a single, fixed idea. Poets, composers, artists, and historians have all played

an important role in shaping nationalist thinking and movements.

Nations usually define themselves by a highly selective—and often imagined—view of the past. In 1882 the French historian Ernest Renan claimed, "getting its history wrong is part of being a nation." Heroes and heroic episodes are remembered, praised, and magnified in importance, while shameful episodes are quietly forgotten. Renan stated that national identity depended on the sense of a shared past: "to have performed great deeds together, to wish to perform still more—these are the essential conditions for being a people."

New nations

The following nations have gained or regained their independence as states since 1990:

1990 Namibia, Yemen
1991 Armenia, Azerbaijan, Belarus, Croatia, Estonia, Georgia, Kazakhstan, Kyrgyzstan, Latvia, Lithuania, Macedonia, Moldova, Slovenia, Tajikistan, Turkmenistan, Ukraine, Uzbekistan
1992 Bosnia and Herzegovina
1993 Eritrea, Slovakia
1994 Palau
2002 East Timor

Newest nation—East Timor, once a Portuguese colony, regained its independence in 2002.

Belonging to a nation (**nationhood**) means that the members of that nation think of themselves as tied both to the past and the future. Some nationalists have believed that what links generations is their actual blood—in other words, that the Greeks or the Spanish, for example, are a distinct race. But the movement of people throughout history means that modern Greeks have little or no genetic connection with the Greeks of ancient Athens and Sparta. And the Spanish people, almost all Catholics, carry the blood of Muslim Arabs, who ruled Spain for seven centuries.

Two types of nationalism

Ethnic nationalism is based on belief in inheritance. It is genetic and historical. It is "closed," because only those sharing the bonds of blood and belonging can be fellow nationals. Civic nationalism is based on the commitment to certain shared values. Civic nationalism is "open," in the sense that anyone can become a full member of society by accepting the duties of a **citizen**.

Civic nationalism ignores claims of blood or race. It is most clearly seen in nations that are made up mainly of immigrants from other countries, such as the United States, Canada, Australia, or Argentina. Newcomers, after living there for a period, make a pledge of allegiance to their new country and swear to obey its laws and thereby become citizens,

New nations built by immigrants, like the U.S., offer citizens the chance to forge new identities.

On being American

In 1900 President Theodore Roosevelt declared:

Americanism is a question of principle, of purpose, of idealism, of character. It is not a matter of birthplace or creed or line of descent.

regardless of their birth or former nationality. About half of all nations permit **dual citizenship,** where a person is a citizen of two states.

Denmark is a small but ancient nation that in the past has ruled Norway, Sweden, and England as well as its own homeland. The Danish flag, flown since the 1200s, is the world's oldest national flag. Above, the Danes turn out in force to cheer their queen.

Patriotism or nationalism?

Patriotism is when love of your own people comes first; nationalism is when hate for people other than your own comes first.
Charles De Gaulle (1890–1970), war hero and president of France

By "patriotism" I mean devotion to a particular place and a particular way of life, which one believes to be the best in the world but has no wish to force on other people.... Nationalism, on the other hand, is inseparable from the desire for power. The abiding purpose of every nationalist is to secure more power and more prestige, not for himself but for the nation.
George Orwell, author of *Animal Farm*, 1945

Scotland

The history of Scotland shows the circular and changing nature of history and nations. It also shows how a sense of national identity and nationalism can be created through conflict, culture, institutions, heroes, poets, and the symbols of **nationhood**.

The first known record of the Picts living in Scotland is from 297 C.E., but they may have been there earlier. The Scots who, like the Picts, spoke a **Celtic** language, invaded southwest Scotland from their home in Ireland about 500 C.E. The Picts and Scots fought, then blended with later arrivals— Vikings from Scandinavia and Anglo-Normans from England. In 843 C.E., Scotland was united under one king, although fighting among rival lords and tribal chiefs continued. When the English king, Edward I (1272–1307), tried to conquer Scotland, the Scots united against him. In 1320, leading Scots signed the Declaration of Arbroath, swearing that as long as there were a hundred of them left alive, they would never surrender to English rule. They adopted the blue-and-white flag of St. Andrew as their national banner.

England finally recognized Scottish independence in 1328. However, border wars and raiding continued until 1603, when James VI of Scotland became James I of England (after the death of the childless Elizabeth I). From 1603 to 1707, Scotland shared a king with

Scots in national dress gather to mark t 700th anniversary of Scotland's victory over the English at Stirling Bridge in 12! Note the cross of St. Andrew flag and, i the background, the red lion flag of the royal house of Stuart.

Scotland—a timeline

843 C.E.	Scotland united under a single king, Kenneth McAlpin
1320	Scottish leaders sign the Declaration of Arbroath
1328	England recognizes Scottish independence
1603	Scotland and England are united under a ruler
1707	The Act of Union abolishes the Scottish parliament
1928	Founding of the National Party of Scotland
1934	National Party of Scotland is renamed the Scottish National Party (SNP)
1979	Scots vote against devolution
1997	Scots vote in favor of devolution
1999	A separate Scottish parliament is restored

England but kept its own **parliament.** Scots settled in Northern Ireland and in the American **colonies.** But after a disastrous attempt to found a colony in Panama brought Scotland to near bankruptcy, the country entered a merger with England.

By the Act of Union of 1707, Scotland abolished its parliament and sent representatives to England instead. Scotland kept its own separate laws, church, and education system. Robert Burns's poems and Sir Walter Scott's novels kept a distinctive Scottish culture alive. Although Scotland kept its identity, the Scots were fully part of Great Britain. Scots made up only 5 percent of the population but 10 percent of Great Britain's army.

A nation once again?

In 1928 the National Party of Scotland was founded to fight for full Scottish independence. But 50 years later, Scottish voters rejected even limited **devolution,** although rivalry with England in sports, especially soccer, remained strong. In 1997 Scots finally voted in favor of devolution. A separate Scottish parliament, with limited powers, was restored —though Scots continue to send members of parliament to England as well. The Scottish National Party still wants complete independence, preferably by 2007, three centuries after the Act of Union.

The Birth of Modern Nationalism

Nationalist elements can be traced back centuries before nationalism fully emerged during the French Revolution of 1789 (see page 19). The Jews of ancient Israel thought of themselves as God's chosen people. Despite being scattered from their homeland for two thousand years, Jews held on to their identity through religious rituals, the use of the Hebrew language in worship and study, and the memory of their history. In 1948, Israel was created as a Jewish state.

These Hasidic Jews are preparing for the holiday of Passover. Rituals like this have enabled the Jews to retain their national identity despite being scattered from their homeland.

Nations invent themselves

...take the Estonians. At the beginning of the 19th century they didn't even have a name for themselves.... They were just a category. Since then they've been brilliantly successful at creating a vibrant culture ... the Ethnographic Museum in Tartu has one object for every ten Estonians and there are only a million of them.

Ernest Gellner, British philosopher, 1995

The inhabitants of the 300 **city-states** that made up ancient Greece took pride in a common culture based on religion, the Greek language, and a passion for sports and discussion. But the Greeks were too divided by local loyalties to become one nation. The only time they united was against Persia, their common enemy. The Greeks were conquered by outsiders, first the Macedonians, and then the Romans in 146 B.C.E.

Developing a national identity

Ancient Rome was a multiethnic empire based not on nationality but on citizenship. Originally only Roman men were **citizens**, with the right to take part in politics. Then citizen rights were given to other members of society, and later to nonmembers if they served in the army. Finally, all adult men under Roman rule were given citizenship, regardless of birth or language, though women and slaves— the majority of the population—were not. In 212 C.E., citizenship was granted to all free-born people.

An emperor and his son parade through Rome in about 40 B.C.E.

For a thousand years after the breakup of the Roman Empire, the strongest political loyalties were local—to a king, lord, or city. Europeans, however, shared a common Christian culture, Catholic in the west and **Orthodox** in the east. From the 1500s onward, the more successful European kingdoms, such as England, Spain, and France, created powerful central governments that imposed greater uniformity in law, religion, and language.

Heretics being burned by the Inquisition in 1739. Captured Protestant British sailors feared they might suffer the same fate.

The emergence of Protestantism in 1517 destroyed the common Catholic culture of Western Europe and gave wars between states the added dimension of religious hatred. Some countries, such as Italy and Spain, remained Catholic, while others, such as England and Sweden, became Protestant. Latin stopped being the common European language of

government and religion and was replaced by English, French, Spanish, and others. This limited the communication between different nations while increasing communication within them. During the 1600s and the 1700s, wars over **territory** and trade further sharpened people's sense of identity as English, French, Spanish, and so on.

The Romantic Movement

The American Revolution in 1775 (see page 16) and the French Revolution in 1789 (see page 19) happened at the same time as the Romantic movement in Europe. The Romantic movement rejected what the intellectuals of the previous century had valued—order, harmony, moderation —in favor of passion, adventure, and struggle. Scholars and writers led the way in rediscovering national "roots" in folklore, legend, and language.

The search for national identity was especially intense in Germany, a nation split up into dozens of small kingdoms and **city-states**. These nevertheless shared a common language and culture. The Brothers Grimm, now remembered for writing fairy tales, were also serious students of the German language and began writing a dictionary. Johann Herder (1744-1803) collected folk songs, wrote about German art, and preached that it was in the common people (the *Volk*) of Germany that the true spirit of the nation (*Volksgeist*) was found. At the University of Berlin in 1807–1808, Johann Fichte (1762–1814) gave a series of lectures in which he argued that German was the language from which all other languages developed. He also claimed that Germans were the world's finest people.

The German philosopher and nationalist Johann Fichte

The United States—a nation by stages

From 1607 onward, British migrants settled on the east coast of what is now the United States and established thirteen separate **colonies**. Each had power over local affairs, but the big questions of war, taxes, and trade were decided by the British Parliament in London. In 1763 some colonial leaders began to argue that British rule was unjust and that the colonies ought to rule themselves.

The American Revolution began with armed rebellion in 1775. At first the rebels were in a minority. At least as many other colonists wanted to remain under British rule. The rest were either undecided or uninterested. As they got caught up in the fighting, however, the colonists came to see British soldiers as foreign oppressors, and they increasingly supported the rebels. France, Britain's traditional enemy, sent soldiers and a navy to support the rebels. The British government finally gave up in 1783 and accepted the independence of the colonies.

Colonial rebels actually lost the Battle of Bunker Hill in 1775, but proved they could inflict severe losses on British professional soldiers. This painting, by the American artist John Trumbull, was done in London more than ten years after the event.

This did not, however, mean that the former colonists all suddenly thought of themselves as members of a new nation. When the leaders of the former colonies—now states—met to draw up a **constitution,** they jealously guarded their powers. The national government was given control of matters such as defense, but states kept control of their own criminal laws and the right to raise taxes. As late as 1849, the senator and former vice-president John C. Calhoun could state that: "We are not a Nation, but a Union. . . of equal and sovereign States."

Gradually, over the course of a century, a strong sense of American national identity emerged. Immigration to the United States from many different countries brought together people from a wide range of backgrounds. As Senator Carl Schurz argued in 1859: "American nationality. . . did not spring from one family, one tribe, one country, but incorporates the vigorous elements of all civilized nations on Earth."

Through schoolbooks and popular celebrations, American nationalism focused on the heroic figures of George Washington, and the **Founding Fathers**, who drew up the U.S. Constitution. This nationalism was expressed in the "Stars and Stripes" of the U.S. flag and in Fourth of July Independence Day celebrations.

Fireworks, seen here in New York in 2002, are a traditional part of the Fourth of July celebrations that celebrate the signing of the Declaration of Independence.

17

During the 1800s settlers in covered wagons migrated westward across the U.S.

American nationalism was strengthened by Noah Webster's dictionary, which honored American English as fully equal to British English. American settlers were called upon to go westward and claim for themselves a country the size of a continent. President John Quincy Adams (1767–1848) declared that America was "destined by God and nature to be the most populous and powerful people." But even after three-quarters of a century of independence, the American sense of shared identity was not strong enough to prevent a civil war (1861–1865), which cost 600,000 lives and was the bloodiest conflict in American history.

It was not until 1863 that Thanksgiving Day became a national holiday and not until after the Civil War that the phrase United States began to be used in the singular rather than the plural (*the* United States,

The Pledge of Allegiance

The Pledge of Allegiance regularly recited in schools was written in 1892 by the Baptist minister Francis Bellamy. Its original wording was: "I pledge allegiance to my Flag and the Republic for which it stands, one nation, indivisible, with liberty and justice for all." Bellamy wanted to include the word equality but left it out because many school superintendents were against equality for women and nonwhites. In 1924 "my flag" was changed to "the flag of the United States of America." In 1954 the phrase "under God" was added. This wording is now being challenged by some people as unconstitutional.

instead of *these* United States). And it was not until 1931 that "The Star-Spangled Banner" became the official national anthem of the United States.

The French Revolution

Modern nationalism emerged during the French Revolution (1789–1815). French support for the American struggle for independence bankrupted France, leading to a crisis in 1789. Critics of the French monarchy argued that political power should flow upward from the people to a government they elected, not downward from a king who claimed to have been chosen by God. The French would no longer be defined by their loyalty to a king but by their loyalty to France.

This loyalty is known as popular **sovereignty**—the idea that only the people of a nation have the right to grant power to a government. In 1789 revolutionaries seized control in France. They executed the king and abolished the monarchy, replacing it with a **republic** in which rulers were elected. They got rid of the old royal flag and adopted a new one. Coins no longer had the image of the king on them but symbols of the republic. Priests and aristocrats lost the right not to pay taxes. All **citizens** were to be equal before the law. The anniversary of the outbreak of the revolution, July 14, became a national holiday.

French Declaration of the Rights of Man and the Citizen (1789)

1. Men are born and remain free and equal in rights.
2. The aim of every political association is the preservation of the natural. . . rights of man. These rights are Liberty, Property, Safety, and Resistance to Oppression.
3. The source of all sovereignty lies essentially in the Nation [that is to say, rightful power comes from the will of the people, not the king].

The declaration also proclaimed the rights of all citizens to equal treatment before the law, participation in politics, and freedom of religion and speech.

Until its replacement by the Euro in 2002, French coins carried the words, *Liberty, Equality, Fraternity*.

Chain reaction in Europe

The French Revolution started a chain reaction of nationalist movements. When armies of French **royalist** exiles and foreign troops invaded France to crush the revolution's leaders, the republic declared that it was the duty of every citizen to defend it with his or her life. As the words of the French national anthem (written in 1792) proclaimed:

Let us go, children of the fatherland,
Our day of glory has arrived.
Against us is tyranny,
The bloody flag is raised; the bloody flag is raised.
Do you hear in the countryside
The roar of these savage soldiers
They come right into our arms
To cut the throats of your sons, your comrades.
To arms, citizens!
Form your battalions,
Let us march, let us march!
That their impure blood
Should water our fields.

Napoleon's troops crossing the Danube River in 1809. Twenty years earlier, the Anglo-Irish thinker Edmund Burke predicted that, although the French Revolution had begun by proclaiming liberty for all, it would end by creating a military dictatorship. He was right.

Napoleon flees after his final defeat at Waterloo. His vision of a united Europe cost more than 1 million lives.

The French successfully pushed back the royalist attack and began to invade neighboring countries to spread republicanism throughout Europe. In most cases, republicanism was rejected because it was imposed by force and was foreign to national traditions. After the fall of the French Emperor Napoleon in 1815, monarchies were restored and political rights were limited to a minority in most countries.

In Germany, however, there was a growing pride in the part Germans had played in defeating Napoleon. Student clubs (*Burschenschaften*) were formed to practice fencing and gymnastics and sing nationalistic songs, such as "What is the German's Fatherland?" (see box).

A nationalist anthem

What is the German's fatherland?
Is it Prussia or the Swabian's land?
Is it where the grape glows on the Rhine?
Where seagulls skim the Baltic's brine?
Oh no! more grand
Must be the German's fatherland!

What is the German's fatherland?
Now name at last that mighty land!
Where'er resounds the German tongue,
Where'er its hymns to God are sung!
That is the land,
Brave German, that thy fatherland!

"What is the German's Fatherland?", written by E. M. Arndt, a history professor, in 1812

Nations and Empires

In the early 1800s, nationalism and idealism seemed to go together. **Idealistic** people in nations that had achieved their independence were often willing to help others gain theirs. Sometimes governments got involved, too. Nations achieved independence—some through their own efforts, some through other states getting involved for their own reasons, and some through a combination of the two. These situations are illustrated in the examples below.

Greece
Between 1821 and 1833, Greece fought for independence from the Turkish **Ottoman Empire**. The Greek struggle was led by a Russian general. It was supported by Romanians and Serbs who were also in revolt against the Ottoman Empire, and by the English poet Lord Byron and a band of British and American volunteers known as the Philhellenes (lovers of Greece). When it looked as if the Turks might reconquer Greece, the British, French, and Russian governments united to sink an Ottoman fleet. They forced the Ottoman ruler to accept Greek independence and grant limited self-rule to the Serbs. The Greeks invited a German prince to become their first king because no Greek was acceptable to all of them.

Fighting to overthrow the rule of their Ottoman rulers, who were Muslim, the Greeks chose Easter Day, the most important date in the Christian calendar, to raise their flag in revolt.

Belgium

Until 1795 Belgium was ruled by Austria. Then it was conquered by France. In 1815 it was handed over to Holland. In 1830 the Belgians rose against Dutch rule. When the Dutch tried to invade, Britain led other states in pressing them to accept Belgian independence, which they finally did in 1839. The British government's main motive was to ensure that a **territory** from which Britain could easily be invaded would become a relatively powerless but independent state.

Poland

Between 1772 and 1795, Poland, once a mighty kingdom stretching from the Baltic Sea to the Black Sea, was carved up among Russia, Austria, and Prussia. After 1815 most Poles were under Russian rule. In 1830 they rose in revolt. No one came to their aid and the revolt was crushed, as was another in 1863. The strength of the Catholic Church and the Polish language, however, kept alive a strong sense of Polish national identity. This persisted against the influence of the Russian language and the Russian **Orthodox** Church, until the collapse of the Russian Empire allowed Poland to become independent once more in 1918.

Pope John Paul II visits his native Poland in 2002. The Pope's own pride in his nation helped sustain Poland's sense of identity during its years under Soviet Communist control (1947-1992).

Unification

In 1848, revolutions against **autocratic** governments broke out in many parts of Western and Central Europe. An attempt to set up a **parliament** for a united Germany failed. So did a short-lived Hungarian **republic.** A congress in Prague demanded **autonomy** (self-government) for the Czechs under Austrian rule, but to no effect. The gaining of national independence by popular uprisings gave way to its achievement by war and diplomacy. The following examples show how different states became unified.

Italy

The unification of Italy became known as the Risorgimento, which means rebirth or resurrection. Its strongest supporters were the urban middle class, and particularly their student sons. Once again, help from outside was crucial. In 1815, northwestern Italy was dominated by the kingdom of Sardinia, which included mainland Piedmont. The northeast (Lombardy and Venice) was occupied by Austria, and the south by the kingdom of the Two Sicilies. The central part was split between the **Papal States** (states controlled by the Vatican) and the small states of Parma, Modena, and Tuscany, which were effectively under Austrian control. Although **republicans** briefly seized power in the cities of Rome, Turin, Florence, and Venice in 1848, their regimes all collapsed.

Count Cavour, prime minister of Piedmont, skillfully gained the support of the French emperor, Napoleon III,

Marching to destiny— Garibaldi leads the Thousand into Palermo, Sicily, in June 1860. The city's people rose up in their support, convincing Count Cavour to lend secret aid.

by offering him the regions of Nice and Savoy in return for military aid against Austria. Austria was defeated in 1859 and left its Italian **territories,** except for Venice. Shortly afterward, Giuseppe Garibaldi and a volunteer army invaded the kingdom of the Two Sicilies and offered its land to the king of Piedmont. Following **plebiscites** (votes) approving his position, Victor Emmanuel II became the first king of a united Italy in 1861. In 1866, Italy supported Germany in a war against Austria and received Venice as its reward.

Giuseppe Garibaldi (1807–1882)

Garibaldi was a sailor's son and a member of a revolutionary movement, Young Italy, that failed to seize power in Genoa in 1834. He fled to South America and fought on behalf of Uruguay against an Argentine invasion. From 1848 to 1849 he fought for the short-lived republics in Rome and Venice. In 1859 he raised a band of volunteers to fight the Austrians. "I offer neither pay . . . nor provisions," he said. "I offer hunger, thirst, forced marches, battles, and death. Let him who loves his country in his heart and not with his lips only, follow me."

Garibaldi's exploits made him a hero on both sides of the Atlantic. In 1860 he called for more volunteers—the Thousand—to help him conquer southern Italy for Piedmont. Many British and other non-Italians felt honored to serve under him. Garibaldi brilliantly defeated the much larger armies sent against him and then retired to live as a farmer, taking no reward or title for himself.

During the Franco-Prussian War of 1870–1871, Garibaldi came out of retirement to lead a volunteer force in defense of the new French republic.

Germany

Germany in the early 1800s consisted of 39 separate kingdoms, **principalities,** and **city-states,** joined together in a loose **confederation.** The largest of these was Prussia, a monarchy with a strong military tradition. The Austrian Empire was its main rival for influence over the other kingdoms. Ruled by a German-speaking minority, the Austrian Empire was a patchwork of a dozen different nationalities.

The German people shared a common language and were drawn together by a union to boost trade among different states. This union purposely excluded Austria. The growth of railroads, the telegraph, postal services, and newspapers also helped break down barriers between Germans.

The German nation was unified by Prussia, under the guidance of its chief minister, Otto von Bismarck (1815–1898). In 1864 Prussia fought Denmark to **annex** the **duchies** of Schleswig and Holstein. In 1866 Prussia proposed reforming the original confederation to exclude Austria. When Austria

In 1864 German troops were welcomed by the German-speaking inhabitants of the formerly Danish-ruled duchies of Schleswig and Holstein.

Warfare gave the armed forces a permanently powerful influence in the politics of the new German nation.

A movement of the young

University students played a leading part in spreading nationalist ideas in Germany, Austria, Italy, and France in the period after 1815. As students, they were interested in ideas. Being young, without work or family ties, they had time for politics. Some were attracted by the excitement of joining secret societies. The German student Heinrich von Gagern wrote to his father to explain the new mood in his university: "For the average student of the past, the university years were a time to enjoy life . . . their university duty was only to avoid failing the examination. . . . But . . . another group . . . has managed to get the upper hand. . . . Their purpose is to make a better future for the Fatherland . . . we want Germany to be considered one land and the German people one people. . . . Regional clubs are forbidden and we live as a German brotherhood."

opposed this, Prussia defeated it in six weeks. Twenty-one German states north of the Main River agreed to join a North German confederation, led by Prussia, with its capital in Berlin, the Prussian capital.

In 1870 Bismarck managed to provoke France into declaring war on Prussia. The southern German states as well as the northern ones were bound by military agreements to support Prussia. In 1871 Prussian victory over France led to all the German states forming a German empire. The Prussian king became its emperor with the title of kaiser (caesar).

27

Building an Empire

In the second half of the 1800s, the growth of education, newspapers, and compulsory **military service** made it possible to spread the idea of "national cultures." The ideas of **nationhood** and nationalism were glorified in art, music, and literature, and especially in the writing of history.

The biologist Charles Darwin (1809–1882) explained the evolution of living things as a process called "natural selection," in which the less-fit species were eliminated in a struggle for survival. Extreme nationalists such as the German general, Friedrich von Bernhardi (1849-1930), applied his theory to politics. "War is a biological necessity," Bernhardi wrote. "Without it an unhealthy development will follow, which excludes every advancement of the race and therefore all real civilization."

Darwinian theories fueled nationalism and were used to justify the building up of overseas empires and **colonies** in Asia, Africa, and the Pacific. It was argued that if nature itself was based on "the survival of the fittest," then it must also be true that the stronger nations had a right to rule over the weaker ones. The German historian, Heinrich von Treitschke (1834–1896) declared that "all great nations in the fullness of their strength have desired to set their mark upon barbarian lands and those who fail to take part in this great rivalry will play a pitiable role in time to come."

The scramble for Africa

Europeans had traded with the people of the African coast for four centuries. However, until the 1860s, their knowledge of the interior of the continent was limited by disease, warlike tribes, and the difficulties of transportation. These problems were solved by the introductions of the drug **quinine**, the machine gun,

Seat of power? British officials lay down the law to local chiefs in East Africa in the days of colonial rule.

and the steamboat. In 1879, Leopold II of Belgium claimed the Congo, a huge part of central Africa. In 1881, France declared that it was taking control of Tunisia. In 1882, British forces occupied Egypt. In 1884, Germany claimed Namibia, Cameroon, Togo, and Zanzibar.

To avoid the possibility of war arising from conflicting claims, the European powers came together at conferences in Berlin (1884) and Brussels (1890). They created borders for the various European colonies. Some of these were just chance lines across the map of the continent. Such borders often sliced through the territories of existing African nations. People who had previously been one nation were now ruled by different colonial powers with different laws and languages. Surprisingly, most of these borders have lasted to the present, with none of the **post colonial** states willing to challenge them.

Anti-imperialism

Nationalism not only fueled **imperialism** but **anti-imperialism** too. Britain's empire was the largest. Movements for national independence challenged British rule through both peaceful and violent means.

Britain colonized India from 1757 onward. Before British rule, the Indian subcontinent had been a patchwork of hundreds of princely states, loosely supervised by the **Mughal** emperor but divided by race, religion, and language. The British introduced railroads, schools, and newspapers, which helped unite India. By introducing the English language, the British provided Indian leaders with a way of communicating with one another. In 1885 the Indian National Congress was founded to press the British to share power with Indians. Later, it would head the mainly peaceful movement for all-out independence (see page 42). Some of the founders of the Congress were themselves British.

A challenge to British rule, often through violent means, emerged in Ireland (see page 37). A constant stream of immigrants to the United States sent back funds and volunteers to support the Fenians, an anti-British terrorist group, which organized bombings and assassinations. Many Irish also rejected British rule in a cultural sense by refusing to play British sports. In 1884 the Gaelic Athletic Association was founded to promote Irish sports such as hurling and handball. Irish intellectuals such as W. B. Yeats began to revive interest in ancient myths and the Gaelic language and to put on plays with Irish themes.

British aristocrats in India hunt tigers with the local rulers. In Asia and Africa, Britain often supported native rulers. These rulers collaborated with the British in order to make their control acceptable to the ruled. Nationalist opponents of British power therefore often tried to overthrow traditional local rulers as well as the British.

A hurling final in Galway, Ireland. Irish people who had served in the British armed forces or police were traditionally banned from taking part in nationalist sports such as hurling.

How Japan became a nation

Europeans first reached Japan in 1543, bringing Christianity with them. Japan was torn by civil war and was unable to resist the newcomers or their faith. But eventually a military **dictatorship** restored order. The dictatorship banned Christianity and, starting in 1639, ended contact with the outside world for fear of foreign interference.

In 1853 a U.S. fleet forced Japan, under threat of bombardment, to open its ports to trade. Japan's leaders knew the great Chinese Empire had been humiliated by the modern armed forces of Britain and France. To avoid the same fate, Japan began a rapid program of modernization, using imported Western experts and technology. The ancient provinces that had been ruled by warlords were abolished, and power was concentrated in the hands of a strong centralized government. A Western-style calendar, coinage, and postal service were introduced. Compulsory education and **conscription** taught the younger generation of Japanese to be loyal and obedient to their emperor. Japan gained the overseas colonies of Taiwan and Korea as a result of swift, successful wars against China and Russia. In 1902, Japan signed a treaty of alliance with Britain. In half a century, Japan had transformed itself from an isolated country into one of the world's most powerful nations.

A Maori performance is staged in New Zealand. New Zealanders of all ethnic backgrounds have come to take pride in the cultural heritage of the Maori.

Peaceful nationalism

Not all forms of nationalism are aggressive. British colonies, such as those of Canada, Australia, and New Zealand, developed their own distinct national identities through the peaceful development of their resource-rich lands. People in these colonies championed their own sports heroes and adapted British customs to a different environment. But all three countries at first failed to bring their **native people** into their new sense of identity.

The histories and languages of the countries of Scandinavia were closely interlinked for 1,000 years, but became more distinct from one another in response to nationalist ideas. Until 1814 Norway was ruled by Denmark, but then it was handed over to Sweden. Although Norway kept its own separate government and **parliament,** the link with Sweden was increasingly resented. Composers such as Edvard Grieg and writers such as Henrik Ibsen made Norwegians proud of their own culture.

Father of Australia

Sir Harry Parkes (1815–1896) urged the Australian colonies to join together as a **federation,** but he died before his goal was achieved. In 1867, he said:

With our splendid harbor, our beautifully situated city, our vast territories, all our varied and inexhaustible natural wealth, if we don't convert our colony into a great and prosperous nation, it will be a miracle of error for which we will have to answer as for a gigantic sin.

In 1905 the Norwegian parliament voted to dissolve the union. After three months of discussion, Sweden accepted this, and Norway and Sweden achieved a peaceful separation. The Norwegians invited a Danish prince to become their king. Finland was part of Sweden until it was conquered by Russia in 1809. The Finns resisted Russian culture through language, religion, and pride in their national composer, Jean Sibelius. They became a separate nation again in 1917.

A new state

Since Roman times, Jewish people had been scattered through many countries, sometimes prospering but often facing persecution. By the late 1800s, half of the world's 10 million Jews lived under Russian rule. Beginning in the 1880s they suffered repeated pogroms (violent, anti-Jewish riots) that led many to emigrate. In 1895 Theodor Herzl, a Jewish journalist and playwright living in Vienna, wrote *Der Judenstaat* (The Jewish State). In it, he argued that Jews should have their own independent country where they could be free and secure. Herzl promoted this belief, known as Zionism, at the first World Zionist Conference, which he organized in 1897. Half a century later, the Zionist dream became a reality with the foundation of Israel in 1948.

The Scandinavian people retain distinct and separate national identities. These children are taking part in a procession to celebrate Norway's national day.

Empires into Nations

Nationalism during the 19th century was largely confined to Europe and mainly took the form of opposition to neighboring peoples. During the 20th century, nationalism extended beyond Europe and concerned various peoples' opposition to rule by Westerners.

In 1901, Winston Churchill (1874–1965), predicted: "The wars of the peoples will be more terrible than those of kings. … A European war can only end in the ruin of the vanquished and the hardly less fatal … exhaustion of the conquerors."

An explosion of nationalism

France's defeat by Prussia in 1870 and 1871 (see page 27) cost it the two eastern provinces of Alsace and Lorraine. This loss was a tremendous blow to national pride. French nationalists dreamed of a war of revenge to recover the provinces. Alsace and Lorraine became part of the new German Empire, which quickly grew into the richest and most powerful state in Europe. France allied itself with Russia. Germany therefore drew closer to Austria-Hungary as a counterweight to Russia. Britain, alarmed at Germany's decision to build a great navy, drew closer to France.

Nationalist hopes and rivalries were most dangerous in the **Balkan** region of southeastern Europe. Like Greece

The fever of war

The Austrian writer Stefan Zweig (1881–1942) described the atmosphere in the Austrian capital, Vienna, on the outbreak of World War I:

I found the city in a tumult … parades in the streets, flags, ribbons, and music burst forth everywhere, young recruits were marching triumphantly, their faces lighting up at the cheering … hundreds of thousands felt … that they belonged together … that they were participating in world history. All differences of class, rank, and language were flooded over.… Each individual … was part of the people and … had been given meaning …They did not know war.… They still saw it through their schoolbooks and paintings in museums … a wild, manly adventure … and the young people were honestly afraid they might miss this most wonderful and exciting experience of their lives … that is why they shouted and sang in the trains that carried them to the slaughter.

(see page 22), the states of Romania, Bulgaria, Serbia, and Montenegro had won their independence from the multinational **Ottoman Empire.** The multinational **Austro-Hungarian Empire** became alarmed at the growth of Serbia. It feared that Serbs still living under Austro-Hungarian rule in Bosnia-Herzegovina might try to break away.

In June 1914, the heir to the Austro-Hungarian throne was assassinated while visiting Sarajevo, the capital of Bosnia-Herzegovina, on Serbia's national day. The assassin was a young Serb who lived in Bosnia. Although the Serbian government denied any involvement, the murder gave Austria-Hungary (with Germany's backing) an excuse to invade Serbia. Russia's decision to aid Serbia then caused the interlocking alliance system to drag France and Britain (known as the Allied Powers) into the struggle. Italy, although allied to Germany and Austria-Hungary (known as the Central Powers), stayed neutral at first. Bulgaria and the Ottomans sided with the Central Powers. This conflict led to World War I.

The Serbian student-nationalist Gavrilo Princip is seized after assassinating Archduke Franz Ferdinand of Austria-Hungary on June 28, 1914.

World War I

Socialists in Germany, France, and Britain believed
that workers, whatever their country of origin, had
far more in common with one another than with
their quarelling rulers. But World War I showed that
the appeal of nationalism was far more powerful than
the unity of workers. When the British government
appealed for soldiers, 750,000 men volunteered in a
month, far more than the army could train, arm, or
even clothe in uniform.

The United States was provoked into joining the war
by German submarine attacks on neutral, especially
American, shipping. President Woodrow Wilson
(1856–1924) had pledged to keep out of the war, but
in 1916 he declared that "the nation's honor is dearer
than the nation's comfort." In 1917 the United States
joined the increasingly exhausted Allied Powers, just
as Russia was slipping into chaos and revolution.
Wilson claimed that America wanted nothing for
itself but to punish German aggression and to free
oppressed nations by granting them self-rule. The
supply of fresh American forces led to the defeat of
the Central Powers. It also meant that Wilson was
able to dominate the postwar Paris peace conference.

Defeat smashed the multiethnic empires of Russia,
Austria-Hungary, and the Ottomans. As Russia
collapsed into revolution, its former provinces of
Poland, Finland, Lithuania, Latvia, and Estonia
declared themselves independent. Austria-Hungary
was split into a separate Austria and Hungary. The
Czechs and Slovaks were joined together to make a
new state, Czechoslovakia. The former **Balkan**
provinces of the empire—Slovenia, Croatia, and
Bosnia-Herzegovina—joined Serbia and Montenegro
to create Yugoslavia. But none of these arrangements
were as neat as they looked on a map.

Ireland reborn—mostly

Ireland's situation illustrated the problem of divided loyalties. About 250,000 Irish people served in the British army during World War I. At the same time, in 1916, with German weapons and support, 2,000 Irish nationalist volunteers launched the unsuccessful Easter Rising in Dublin against British rule. The British crushed the rebels in a week, during which 794 civilians and 521 police and troops were killed. Then the British government made a major mistake by executing fifteen of the leaders. This turned the rebels into martyrs and rallied widespread Irish support for the nationalist cause.

Ireland became increasingly ungovernable as nationalists waged a **guerrilla** war against British forces. In 1922 the British government agreed to separate the country in two, keeping only the six Protestant-dominated counties of Ulster and recognizing the other 26 counties as an independent Irish Free State (now the Republic of Ireland).

Peace, Bread, Land—in 1917, the Communist revolutionary Lenin tempted the war-weary subjects of the tsar with the promise of a new beginning.

The postwar peace conferences only partly accepted the principle of **self-determination.** Not all Hungarians were in the new Hungary. Some found themselves under Polish or Romanian rule. Large numbers of Germans were in Czechoslovakia or Poland or Lithuania. Koreans protesting against Japan's takeover of Korea were ignored, as was the Pan-African Congress, which wanted freedom from European **colonial rule**.

Fascism

Italy, which joined the Allied Powers in 1915 to gain **territory** from Austria-Hungary, lost 300,000 soldiers in World War I and gained very little. National frustration joined with the fear that the **Communist** takeover of Russia (1917–1922) would turn into revolution throughout Europe. This sense of unease built support for a new extreme nationalist movement led by the ex-journalist, Benito Mussolini (1883-1945). The movement was known as **Fascism.**

Mussolini came to power in 1922, but he gradually built up a **dictatorship** in Italy. Meanwhile in defeated Germany, the ex-soldier Adolf Hitler (1889-1945), an Austrian by birth and an admirer of Mussolini, recruited supporters to his own form of Fascism, called Nazism.

Both Italian Fascism and German Nazism promised to set their nations on a path to glory and prosperity by waging war against internal and external enemies. These extreme forms of nationalism suppressed opposition in the name of the unity, discipline, and sacrifice they demanded. Mussolini thought in terms of a colonial empire in Africa, and brutally conquered Ethiopia in 1936. Hitler's main aim was to unite all Germans under his leadership in a single state and use it to conquer a vast empire in the east, reducing Slavic peoples to slavery and, eventually, to extinction.

From his podium, Benito Mussolini gives the Fascist salute. Fascist governments relied on rituals, propaganda, uniforms, slogans, and displays of military might to build support.

The Soviet Union

The Communist revolution in Russia led to the creation of the Union of Soviet Socialist Republics (USSR, also known as the Soviet Union) out of the wreckage of the Russian Empire. In theory, its different **republics** were to be equal with one another. They were to be bound together by the shared Communist ideal of a unity of working people that extended beyond national loyalties. In practice, the USSR was dominated by Russia and the Russian language. It allowed and even encouraged national minorities to express their culture in harmless forms, such as folk dancing, but ruthlessly oppressed religion and any challenge to governmental power.

Mustafa Kemal (1880–1938)

An Ottoman army officer, Kemal fought during World War I and defeated a Greek invasion afterward to become a national hero. He saw the breakup of the **Ottoman Empire** as the chance to build a new Turkey out of its ruins. As the first president of the Turkish republic, Kemal modernized the Turkish language and education, built up industry, gave women the right to vote and encouraged European-style clothes and customs. A new capital, Ankara, was built in the Turkish heartland. All Turks were told "Be Proud You Are Turkish!" and were instructed to take a second Turkish name. Kemal chose Ataturk, which means "Father Turk." Although he crushed opposition to his reforms, Ataturk was respected as a great patriot. His picture is still seen everywhere in Turkey.

The Turkish leader Mustafa Kemal promoted change by his own example, always wearing Western suits or uniforms rather than traditional Muslim clothes.

A world at war

In 1938 German troops **annexed** Hitler's homeland, Austria. Hitler then demanded that the 3 million Germans living in Czechoslovakia come under German rule. Rather than fight, Britain and France agreed that German-speaking territory should be detached from Czechoslovakia. Czechoslovakia had no option but to accept this.

In March 1939, Hitler annexed the rest of Czechoslovakia and seized the former Prussian port of Memel from Lithuania. Seeing that Hitler could not be bought off, Britain and France then guaranteed to help Poland if Germany attacked it. When German troops invaded Poland shortly afterward, in September 1939, World War II began.

Invading German armies posed as "national liberators" in Slovakia (where the Slovaks resented the Czechs), Croatia (where the Croats resented the Serbs), and the Ukraine (where the Ukrainians resented the Russians). The Germans allowed them to set up their own governments. In theory, these were independent; in practice, they were just a way of organizing soldiers and supplies to support the German war effort.

Hitler reviewing uniformed Nazi supporters. Parades and rallies were a dramatic way of demonstrating to the public the strength of support for Nazism.

Japan, meanwhile, took advantage of the defeats suffered by Britain, France, and the Netherlands in Europe to conquer their **colonies** in Southeast Asia, likewise posing as a national liberator and declaring "Asia for the Asians." Although the Japanese did help local nationalists, in reality their occupation of former European colonies proved far more cruel than **colonial rule.**

German troops invading Poland in 1939. Germany's search for *Lebensraum* **(living space) in Eastern Europe finally ended with the displacement of 12 million Germans as refugees.**

In defeating the German invasion, USSR forces annexed the independent Baltic republics of Estonia, Latvia, and Lithuania. Following the defeat of Germany in 1945, the USSR set up a **Communist** government in the eastern part of Germany that its troops controlled. It also helped local Communists take power in Poland, Czechoslovakia, Hungary, Romania, and Bulgaria. In Albania and Yugoslavia, local Communist fighters took power after defeating the invading Italians and Germans.

Decolonization

The long-term effect of World War II was the weakening of the British, French, and Dutch empires. They were forced to abandon their **colonies.** The war had cost them huge sums of money and their people were more interested in rebuilding their lives at home than in fighting to hold onto colonies abroad. From the 1940s to the 1960s, throughout Asia and Africa, these colonies became independent states.

Britain's Indian Empire split into India, Pakistan, and the Buddhist Burma (Myanmar). The decision over Kashmir, a Muslim state under a Hindu ruler, joining India has led to conflict between India and Pakistan ever since. In Palestine, the British empire failed to balance the rights of Jewish immigrants with those of local Arabs. After a 1947 decision by the United Nations to partition the territory between Jews and Arabs, the Jewish people were left to fight for an independent Israel, which was established in 1948.

France fought to hang onto Vietnam until defeat in 1954. France also held onto Algeria until 1962, when it quit after a war that cost 500,000 lives. In Indonesia, the Dutch were similarly beaten by a nationalist **guerrilla** campaign, and recognized Indonesian independence in 1949.

In much of Africa, the withdrawal of a colonial power sometimes removed the most important factor

The Htoo twins

Burmese people account for two-thirds of the population of Myanmar. The largest of many minorities is the Karen people, some of whom have been fighting for a separate Karen state ever since Myanmar became independent from British rule in 1948. Burmese army counterattacks have forced tens of thousands of Karens over the border into refugee camps in Thailand. By 1997, only a few thousand Karen guerrillas were left fighting. Then a band of 200, calling itself God's Army, began to win against the Burmese under the leadership of twelve-year-old twins, Luther and Johnny Htoo. Their followers thought they had magic powers that protected them in battle and guaranteed victory. They obeyed the twins' orders not to swear, drink, gamble, or eat pork. In 2001, however, the Htoo twins gave up fighting and fled to a refugee camp in Thailand.

uniting its former subjects. Leaders of new states competed for power by appealing to tribal or regional loyalties. This resulted in civil wars in many countries on the continent.

Throughout Asia and Africa, especially in the 1960s, movements for national independence promised equality, planning, and modernization for all **citizens** of the future new nations. But these promises were rarely kept. The new **post colonial** nations were usually desperately short of trained managers, doctors, and teachers, and often depended for their prosperity on the success and price of a few key crops or raw materials. Corruption, unrealistic ambitions, and rivalries between ethnic and religious groups have often combined to produce instability in such nations.

Lord Mountbatten, the last British viceroy, is cheered as India gains its independence in 1948.

Mohandas Gandhi (1869–1948)

Gandhi trained as a lawyer in England and settled in South Africa, where his struggle for the rights of Indian immigrants made him known as Mahatma or "Great Soul." Returning to India in 1914, Gandhi accepted British rule until a massacre of peaceful demonstrators in 1919 led him to launch a movement of nonviolent resistance. His methods included strikes, nonpayment of taxes, refusal to buy British goods, and hunger strikes. Gandhi hoped the common struggle against British rule would unite India's Hindu majority and its Muslim minority into one people. He was deeply saddened when British rule ended with separation into a Hindu-dominated India and a Muslim-dominated Pakistan, with the loss of half a million lives in Hindu-Muslim riots. Gandhi was shot dead by a Hindu because of his sympathy with Muslims. Gandhi's nonviolent methods were an inspiration for the U.S. civil rights movement of the 1950s and 1960s.

Nationalism and Communism

To many of its followers, **Communism** seemed
to offer the promise of an idea that was bigger and
better than nationalism. It promised a world in
which people everywhere would work together for
the benefit of all. But, in practice, **Communist**
governments often manipulated nationalist feelings
to create hatred and fear among people.

From the 1940s until the breakup of the USSR in
1991, world politics was dominated by a conflict
known as the Cold War. On one side stood the
United States and its allies, on the other side stood
the USSR and its allies. In theory, Communism
promised a future world in which the unity of
working people would make national frontiers
meaningless. In practice, Communist states usually
imposed tight border security to prevent their people
from leaving and to control contact with the outside
world. Nationalist resistance to Communism led to
failed uprisings in East Germany in 1953,
in Hungary in 1956, and in Czechoslovakia in
1968. These uprisings were suppressed by Soviet
armed forces, and, as a result, thousands were driven
into **exile.**

**In 1968 Russian tanks
entered Prague to crush
Czech reforms for
greater freedom. The
invading troops were
bewildered when they
were not welcomed.**

Cult of personality

In theory, Communist states, inspired by the same ideas, should have been very similar. In practice, they kept distinct national characteristics. Communism stressed that all working people were of equal value. The strictly controlled art and literature of Communist states presented the workers as heroic figures in paintings, posters, films, and ballets. But several Communist states also presented their leaders as figures of genius whose pictures and statues were seen everywhere and whose sayings and doings filled newspapers, television programs, and schoolbooks. This "cult of personality" is something many dictatorships share.

In the USSR the "cult of personality" began with the leader of the revolution, Lenin (1870–1924), and reached its height under his successor, Stalin (1879–1953). It was copied by the Chinese leader Mao Zedong (1893–1976) and to a lesser extent in Vietnam by Ho Chi Minh (1890–1969). Cuba has been dominated by its Communist leader, Fidel Castro (1926–) ever since he took power in 1959. The cult of personality was most evident in Romania with Nicolae Ceausescu (1918–1989), in Albania with Enver Hoxha (1908–1985) and, above all, in North Korea (see box below).

Fidel Castro has ruled Cuba since he seized power in 1959.

Like father, like son

The cult of personality became most extreme in North Korea. The "Great Leader" Kim Il Sung (1912–1994) was presented as the hero who had freed Korea from Japanese rule and transformed the country into a modern industrial power. In reality, his spending on weapons and grand buildings brought the country to ruin. But this did not prevent his son, "Dear Leader" Kim Jong Il (1942–) from succeeding him. Seven years of famine in the 1990s killed 2 million people, but North Korea remains isolated from the rest of the world and under Kim's control.

Although **Communist** states claimed to cooperate unselfishly with one another to build a better world, they actually behaved according to their own national interests. In 1949 Communists took power in China and relied heavily on the USSR to help them build up modern industries. But within ten years, China had quarreled with the USSR about how a Communist country should be run, and the USSR withdrew its experts and support. The two countries increasingly became rivals rather than partners.

Tito successfully balanced the rivalries of Serbs, Croats, and other nations in Yugoslavia.

When the USSR allied itself with India and supplied it with weapons, China did the same for India's rival, Pakistan. North Vietnam relied on Chinese weapons and support to reunite North and South Vietnam by force between 1954 and 1975. When the reunited Vietnam invaded neighboring Cambodia in 1978, China disapproved and punished it by devastating Vietnam's northern border in 1979. Vietnam therefore switched to the USSR for its weapons, providing use of a former United States naval base in exchange.

Nationalisms revived
Under the ex-**guerrilla** commander Tito (1892–1980), Yugoslavia refused to follow the USSR in its dealings with other nations, traded freely with non-Communist countries, and welcomed foreign tourists. Unlike most Communist governments, it allowed factories and farms to run themselves. Internal politics was based on a careful balancing act as Tito played off different national groups—Serbs, Croats, Bosnians, and Slovenes—against one another. This system outlasted Tito's rule by a decade, but ended in catastrophe as **Communism** was abandoned in favor of reestablishing separate national groupings. In 1991 Slovenia and Macedonia broke away from Yugoslavia almost bloodlessly. But when

Croatia in 1991 and Bosnia-Herzogovina in 1992 aimed for independence, Serbia began a war that cost 250,000 lives before it accepted that the former Yugoslavia had been reduced to only Serbia and Montenegro.

From 1989–1991 the breakup of the USSR led to nationalist revivals throughout Eastern Europe, as Communist governments were overthrown. It also brought about the reunification of East and West Germany and the creation of new, independent states in the **Caucasus** and Central Asia.

In 1989 the Berlin Wall—the symbol of Germany's division into West and East—was finally torn down.

A nation suppressed

Tibet's identity rests on its language and a distinctive form of Buddhism. The nation's spiritual leader is the Dalai Lama. In 1720, China incorporated Tibet into its empire but did not try to impose Chinese culture. When the Chinese Empire collapsed in 1911, Tibet declared its independence and expelled all Chinese. After the Communist takeover of China in 1949, the new Chinese government laid claim to the ancient borders of its empire and invaded Tibet in 1950 and 1951.

The influx of Chinese soldiers and migrants and the suppression of Buddhism provoked a Tibetan uprising in 1959. The Dalai Lama and more than 50,000 followers were forced into **exile** in India, where they remain. In theory, the local government, staffed and headed by Tibetans has autonomy. In practice, power rests with the Chinese Communist Party, headed by the Chinese, with all major decisions approved in Beijing. China continues to rely on military occupation to enforce its rule. The exiled Dalai Lama has said that because Tibet is poor, it would be better off as part of a rapidly prospering country like China. But he wants China to withdraw its soldiers and leave the Tibetans free to follow their religion and their own way of life. The plight of Tibetan refugees and of Tibet itself has attracted the concern of Westerners, such as the pop star Bono and the actor Richard Gere, who campaign against Chinese human rights abuses.

Beyond the Nation-State

Conflict—both within and between countries—has often occurred because the supposed boundaries of nations and the actual borders of states are not the same. Different nations may disagree about where their frontiers are. This has led to repeated conflicts. Argentina lays claim to the Falkland Islands (Las Malvinas), which have been occupied by British settlers since 1833. In 1982 Argentina invaded the Falklands and was forced out by the British. In 1990 the Iraqi dictator Saddam Hussein (1937–) invaded oil-rich Kuwait, claiming it was part of Iraq. The United States led a coalition that restored Kuwait.

Another type of challenge can arise from movements that want to unite existing states in the name of a larger nation. Such movements include Pan-Slavism, Pan-Arabism, Pan-Africanism, and Pan-Europeanism. Some people believe that these movements require states to give up their individuality in favor of a larger sense of identity.

Kuwait following the Gulf War of 1991. Saddam Hussein claimed Kuwait as a "lost province" of Iraq. He invaded Kuwait, but was driven back by an alliance led by the United States. Saddam instructed the retreating Iraqi army to set fire to Kuwaiti oil wells, causing great devastation.

Pan-Slavism

Pan-Slavism was the belief that speakers of Slavic languages, such as Russian, Czech, and Bulgarian, make up a distinct civilization and should form a **confederation** of states. During the 19th century, Pan-Slavism provided an excuse for Russia to interfere in the politics of the **Balkans.** In 1876 Bulgaria, then an Ottoman province, rose in a revolt that was brutally suppressed. In 1877 and 1878 Russia fought and defeated the Ottomans, partly to show Pan-Slavic support for Bulgaria and partly to continue its long-term aim of weakening the **Ottoman Empire.** Bulgaria became a kingdom with an imported German monarch. It became fully independent in 1908, and other Ottoman Balkan **territories** became the independent Romania, Serbia, and Montenegro.

Pan-Arabism

Pan-Arabism is the belief that states in the Arab world should unite to form a confederation. It ignores the fact that the Arab world also contains many Berbers, Turks, and Kurds (who are not Arabs), as well as Jews, Muslim Arabs, Christian Arabs, Armenians, and Copts. Attempts have been made to unite two existing Arab states as a first step. But these have failed in practice. Egypt and Syria, which do not even share a border, agreed to merge in 1958 but angrily proclaimed their separation in 1961. Colonel Qaddafi of Libya has repeatedly offered mergers with other Arab states, but none has been tried seriously.

Even if some states did unite successfully and national minorities could be reassured that their rights would be respected, there remains the problem that some states have different political systems. For example, Algeria, Syria, and Yemen are **republics**, whereas Jordan, Morocco, Oman, Kuwait, Saudi Arabia, and the United Arab Emirates are monarchies.

The League of Arab States

One outcome of Pan-Arabism was the formation of
the League of Arab States in 1945. This has promoted
useful cooperation between states in such areas as
telecommunications, postal services, and banking. But
the League has been divided over attitudes to the
USSR, Iraq's 1990 invasion of Kuwait, extreme
Islamic movements, and ideas about the best way to
support Palestinians in Israel.

Pan-Africanism

Pan-Africanism grew out of a series of six congresses
of African intellectuals and **political activists** that
were held in cities outside Africa between 1900 and
1945. These congresses pressed and planned for the
independence of African **colonies** from European
rule. In calling the first Conference of Independent
African States in Ghana in 1958, the Ghanaian leader
Kwame Nkrumah (1909–1972) hoped to launch a
further movement that would unite the continent
under his leadership. For a few years, Ghana's
prosperity enabled him to cut a big figure on the
world stage. But Ghana was a small country and
was soon ruined by Nkrumah's extravagant dreams
to make it a modern industrial power overnight.
Nigeria, Ghana's oil-rich West African neighbor, was
not likely to put itself under Ghanaian leadership
when it had only just won its own independence
from British rule. It was even less likely that former
French-speaking colonies would be willing to join
an English-speaking community.

A more practical beginning was the foundation in
1963 of the Organization of African Unity (OAU).
The OAU has tried to settle disputes and promote
cooperation among its 53 member states. At a
meeting of the OAU in July 2002, members voted to
reestablish it as the African Union, organized along
the same lines as the European Union (EU).

Pan-Europeanism

Supporters of the European Union, who hope that one day its members will merge into a European superstate, are believers in a form of Pan-Europeanism. However, the newly independent Eastern European countries that want to join the EU have only recently escaped suppression by **Communist** governments. They are uninterested in giving up their national identities. More established European countries also have strong national identities unlikely to be rejected in favor of Pan-Europeanism.

Uniting Europe

We must free ourselves from thinking in terms of nation states…. The countries of Western Europe are no longer in a position to protect themselves individually; not one of them is any longer in a position to salvage Europe's culture.

Konrad Adenauer (1876–1967), chancellor of West Germany, 1953.

Prior nations

Some groups of people claim to have been nations since before the modern idea of nationalism emerged. But it is not clear whether, for example, Native Americans should be thought of as a single nation or as a group of separate nations such as the Iroquois. Canada's First Nations, Australia's Aboriginals, or New Zealand's Maoris also raise this question. Before European settlement, each of these separate groups spoke different languages and fought among themselves. But some argue that the common experience of being pushed aside and then left behind has given **native people** a common history more powerful in uniting them than whatever divided them in the past. In practice, however, these are not nationalist groups because most of their members want fair treatment within their existing state rather than to develop a separate, independent nation.

In 1992 Native Americans used the 500th anniversary of Columbus's arrival in the Americas as an opportunity to protest for their rights.

Countries in conflict

Some nationalist movements aim to break out of existing states in order to achieve independence. In the **Caucasus,** for example, Abkhazia and South Ossetia are seeking to break away from Georgia. Nagorno-Karabakh wants to break away from Azerbaijan, and Chechnya is fighting an occupying Russian army.

The following are examples of groups that challenged an existing state to establish themselves as new, independent nations, hoping to achieve greater justice and security for themselves. They also show how nationalism can lead to the large-scale destruction of human life.

Small nations have often successfully defied powerful empires—at a price. Here, Chechen fighters take on Russian troops in January 1995.

Nigeria and Biafra

In 1960 Nigeria became independent from British rule. Its three regions were dominated by different peoples—the Christian and Muslim speakers of Yoruba in the west, the Muslim speakers of Hausa in the north, and the Christian speakers of Ibo in the east. The discovery of oil off the coast of the eastern region meant it could grow much richer than the other regions as an independent state, keeping the oil wealth to itself. In January 1966, a group of Ibo army officers murdered Nigeria's prime minister and the chief ministers of the northern and western regions. In September, tens of thousands of Ibo living in the northern region were massacred by mobs. A million people fled back to the Ibo homeland, which began to expel non-Ibo people. In May 1967, the eastern region, led by Colonel Ojukwu, declared that it was breaking away from Nigeria to become the independent **Republic** of Biafra. A three-year civil war followed, which cost up to 1 million lives before the devastated eastern region was forced to abandon its bid for freedom.

Bangladesh

When British rule over India ended in 1947, the two large areas in which Muslims made up the majority of the population formed a separate new state of Pakistan. The two areas were about 932 miles (1,500 kilometers) apart. West Pakistan was bigger and richer, and its people spoke Urdu. East Pakistan had a larger, Bengali-speaking, population. The people of East Pakistan believed that West Pakistan was taking more than its fair share of taxes and top jobs. In 1971, East Pakistan declared its independence as Bangladesh, which means "Free Bengal." When armed forces loyal to West Pakistan resisted, a civil war erupted in which the Bengalis were aided by the powerful Indian army. It suited India to divide its neighbor into two smaller states, so an independent Bangladesh was born.

East Timor

Until 1974 Portugal controlled the eastern half of
the island of Timor. However, a military takeover in
Portugal itself offered the Timorese the chance to
seize their independence. After a brief civil war
between pro- and anti-independence groups, East
Timor declared its independence. It was then invaded
and taken over by neighboring Indonesia. The
Indonesians imported settlers to swamp the Catholic,
Portuguese-speaking Timorese with a Muslim,
Indonesian-speaking majority. Tension continued
until the deadlock was unexpectedly broken by the
fall of the government of General Suharto in
Indonesia. To resolve the Timor problem, Suharto's
successor in 1999 allowed a **plebiscite** in which
78.5 percent of Timorese opted for independence.
The local Indonesian military then armed Indonesian
settlers to fight this decision. Thousands of people
were killed and 250,000 Timorese were driven into
temporary **exile.** In September 1999, a UN military
force restored order. A UN temporary government
then organized the move to full independence, which
was achieved on May 20, 2002.

Sri Lanka

Three-quarters of the people of Sri Lanka speak
Sinhalese and the majority are Buddhist. There is also
a Tamil-speaking, mostly Hindu minority. Since the
mid-1980s, militia forces known as the Tamil Tigers
have fought to establish a Tamil homeland—Tamil
Eelam—in Jaffna, a peninsula at the northeastern tip
of Sri Lanka. More than 60,000 have died in the
conflict; 100,000 Tamils have fled to India and
200,000 have fled to the West. Tiger militias have
recruited hundreds of fighters, some as young as
twelve, in the refugee camps. In February 2002, the
government and rebels agreed to a cease-fire to pave
the way for peace talks.

**Tamil Tigers in training in
Sri Lanka in 1995. Some
recruits were as young
as twelve.**

Kurdistan

There are more than 20 million Kurds living in Kurdistan, a mountainous area of land split among Turkey, Iraq, Iran, and Syria. The Kurds have fought for an independent state because of the oppression they have suffered at the hands of others, especially Iraq and Turkey. Iraq has executed perhaps as many as 100,000 Kurdish people. Iraq's defeat in the 1991 Gulf War led to an Iraqi-Kurdish uprising. It failed and led to 2 million Kurds being without a home. As a result, the United States and its allies declared and successfully protected with air patrols a "safe haven" in northern Iraq. Although the safe haven is split into two separate regions run by rival Kurdish political parties, the area is effectively self-governing.

Nationalism—
Today and Tomorrow

Nationalism still fuels conflicts within developed
nations, and not only those with colonial pasts.

Spain

Two million Basques live in northeast Spain and
200,000 live in southwest France. The Basque
language, Euskara, has no similarities with any other
known language. The Basques claim to be directly
descended from the Cro-Magnon cave dwellers who
lived in their region 20,000 years ago; but they have
never had an independent state of their own. And the
name they give to their homeland—Euskadi, which
means "Euskara-speakers united"—was only invented
in the late 1800s.

In Spain the dictator General Franco (1892–1975)
abolished the regional governments in Catalonia and
the Basque provinces and suppressed the Catalan and
Basque languages. Following his death, the country
was divided into 17 self-governing regions. This
satisfied the Catalans but not an extremist Basque
minority.

For Basque nationalists, language is the basis of
Basque identity, although only a third of all Basques
actually speak it. Since 1979, Basque has been
taught in schools, and now 90 percent of Basque
children are learning the language. In 1980 a
Basque **parliament** was elected to govern the
provinces of Vizcaya (Bizkaia), Alava (Araba), and
Guipuzcoa (Gipuzkoa).

Within this region, Basque is recognized as an official
language alongside Spanish. Since 1968 the Basque

**Following the flag—a
Basque nationalist
demonstration.**

separatist organization, ETA (Euskadi ta Askatasuna, meaning "Basque Nation and Liberty"), has used terrorism to press for a separate Basque state. More than 800 people have been killed, including a prime minister of Spain. While ETA has fewer than 40 active terrorists, many more supporters are willing to provide shelter, supplies, or information.

France

French government became highly **centralized** after the revolution in 1789. The armed forces, courts, and schools were required to use the French language and ignore local languages, such as Breton, Cedilla, Provençal, Alsatian, or Corsican. Until the 1980s, officials could refuse to register the births of children who had been given Breton or Basque first names. Since then, official attitudes have reversed so that government now supports the preservation and teaching of these languages.

Regionalist movements in France challenge the power of the central government. This has erupted in violence in Corsica, with the murder of some 220 French officials and police officers since 1976. Many people in France fear that conceding any sort of special status to Corsica, let alone full independence, will only encourage other minorities, such as Bretons and Basques, to raise demands, threatening the unity of the French state.

Canada

The first Europeans to settle in Canada were French. Under British rule after 1763, Canada became overwhelmingly English speaking. French speakers remained concentrated in Quebec, where change was slow in a society of small farmers dominated by the Catholic Church. During the 20th century, as towns and modern industry grew, they did so under the control of English speakers in Quebec.

Between 1960 and 1966, the Liberal Party took control of the Quebec provincial government and set up state-owned enterprises headed by French speakers. Under the leadership of the Parti Quebecois (PQ), founded in 1968, laws were passed in Quebec giving local preference to French. Canada's federal government agreed to make French equal with English as a national language and pledged to protect the rights of French speakers outside Quebec. The PQ continued to insist that Quebec was more than just a "distinct society"; it was a nation. In 1980 Quebec voters rejected a call for complete independence from Canada. In 1995, 49.5 percent voted in favor of independence. Clearly more Quebecois are starting to be in favor of separation.

Bloc Quebecois leader Lucien Bouchard waves to his supporters during a "Yes" rally in favor of independence in Montreal, Canada, on October 25, 1995.

No solution in sight?

Two other nationalist confrontations seem to be without solution. In Northern Ireland, which is still ruled by Britain, the British and Irish governments have agreed to create a power-sharing system. This means that the nationalist/**republican** minority, many of whom wish to unite Northern Ireland with the Republic of Ireland, and the unionist/loyalist majority, who mostly want to remain part of Britain both have a part in local government. Both British and Irish governments have also pledged that no change will be made without a clear vote in favor by a majority of the population of Northern Ireland.

In the Middle East, Israel and Palestine remain locked in a cycle of violence. Palestinians forced from their homeland during Israel's 1948 war of independence use terrorism to demand an independent state in Gaza and the West Bank area. Israel uses its armed forces to punish terrorism and continues to build

A Palestinian woman and her child watch as Israeli forces use bulldozers to demolish Palestinian homes in retaliation for terrorist attacks in April 2002.

new settlements in Palestinian territory. Leading Western powers and the main Arab states agree that Palestinians must have a state and Israel's right to exist within secure borders must be accepted. After so much hatred has built up between Israelis and Palestinians, the problem is either side trusting the other enough to accept a peaceful solution.

Working together

Many of the world's problems, such as the environment, finance, drugs, AIDS, and terrorism, cannot be confined within national boundaries and can only be tackled effectively by nations working together. The increasing movement of populations and global access to information through the Internet challenge the notion of fixed national identities. The likelihood is that we will all increasingly learn to live across borders, rather than simply within them.

Nationalism as a habit

The established nations are those states that have confidence in their own continuity.... The political leaders of such nations—whether France, the United States, the United Kingdom, or New Zealand —are not typically termed nationalists. However ... in so many little ways, the citizenry are daily reminded of their national place in a world of nations ... this reminding is so familiar that it is not consciously registered ... nationalism is not a flag which is being consciously waved with fervent passion; it is the flag hanging unnoticed on the public building.

Michael Billig, Professor of Social Science, Loughborough University, Britain

Timeline

c. 1745	The first national anthem "God Save the King" (Britain)
1776	American Declaration of Independence
1789	French Revolution and Declaration of the Rights of Man and the **Citizen**
1807-1808	Fichte's "Addresses to the German Nation"
1815	Defeat of Napoleon
1830	Revolution in France sparks off nationalist uprisings in Belgium (successful), Italian cities (failed), and Poland (failed)
1848	Revolutions throughout Europe (failed)
1853	Japan forced into contact with the outside world
1859	France and Piedmont liberate Italian **territory** from Austrian rule
1863	Failed nationalist uprising in Poland
1866	Prussia defeats Austria. Venice passes to Italy.
1867	British **colonies** in North America join together as the self-governing Dominion of Canada
1870-1871	Franco-Prussian War leads to establishment of the German empire
1877-1878	Russo-Turkish War establishes independence of Serbia, Montenegro, and Romania
1884	Berlin conference establishes colonial borders in Africa. Gaelic Athletic Association founded.
1885	Indian National Congress founded
1897	First World Zionist Congress held in Basel, Switzerland
1900	Pan-African Congress held in London
1901	Commonwealth of Australia established by former British colonies
1905	Norway breaks away peacefully from Sweden

1914-1918	World War I
1916	Irish Nationalist Easter Rising in Dublin
1917-1922	Russian Revolution and civil war establishes the Union of Soviet Socialist Republics (USSR, Soviet Union). Former Russian provinces reclaim independence as Poland, Finland, Estonia, Latvia, and Lithuania.
1919	Paris Peace Conference; Pan-African Congress held in Paris
1920	Foundation of the League of Nations
1921	Pan-African Congress held in London
1922	Mussolini comes to power in Italy. Partition of Ireland.
1923	Pan-African Congress held in London
1927	Pan-African Congress held in New York
1928	Scottish National Party established
1931	United Staes adopts "The Star-Spangled Banner" as its national anthem
1933	Hitler comes to power in Germany
1939-1945	World War II
1945	United Nations establishes Pan-African Congress held in Manchester, England. Arab League founded
1947	Partition of India and Pakistan
1948	Establishment of the state of Israel
1949	The Netherlands recognizes independence of Indonesia. **Communists** take power in China.
1950	Israel's Law of Return guarantees citizenship for overseas Jews
1953	Failed anti-Communist uprising in East Germany
1954	France recognizes independence of Vietnam

Further Reading

1956	Failed anti-Communist uprising in Hungary
1957	Gold Coast (Ghana) becomes the first British colony in Africa to achieve independence. Rome treaties establish the European Economic Community, forerunner of the European Union.
1959	Fidel Castro takes power in Cuba. Tibetan uprising against Chinese rule.
1962	France recognizes independence of Algeria
1963	Organization of African Unity founded
1967-1970	Biafran breakaway from Nigeria defeated
1968	Failed anti-Communist uprising in Czechoslovakia. Parti Quebecois founded in Quebec, Canada.
1971	East Pakistan breaks away to become Bangladesh
1975	North and South Vietnam reunited
1989-1991	Breakup of the USSR
1992-1994	Bosnia-Herzegovina fights for independence
1993	Czechoslovakia splits peacefully into the Czech Republic and Slovakia
1997	Scotland and Wales vote for devolution
2002	East Timor becomes independent

Cozic, Charles P. *Nationalism and Ethnic Conflict*. Farmington Hills, Mich: Gale Group, 1994.

Katz, Samuel M. *National Liberation Movements*. Minneapolis, Minn: Lerner Publishing, 2003.

Woolf, Alex. *21st Century Debates: Terrorism*. Chicago: Raintree, 2003.

Glossary

annex   take over a territory

anti-imperialism   opposition to being ruled by a foreign country as part of its empire

Austro-Hungarian Empire   multiethnic empire of central and southeastern Europe ruled by members of the Habsburg family until its collapse in 1918. The politically powerful Austrians and Hungarians dominated a dozen other groups of people, including Czechs, Slovaks, Slovenes, and Croats.

autocratic   rule by a single person

autonomy   self-rule, especially in matters of culture such as language

Balkans   mountainous region of southeastern Europe, between Hungary and Greece

Caucasus   mountainous region between Europe and Asia, specifically between the Black Sea and the Caspian Sea

Celtic   member of a culture based on a related group of languages including Gaelic, Welsh, Irish (Erse), Cornish, and Breton

centralize   to favor greater power for central rather than local government

citizen   member of a state with full political rights (e.g., to vote) and duties

city-state   state consisting of a single major city and the surrounding area from which it drew much of its population, food supply, and raw materials

colonial rule   government over a territory by an outside state

colony   new territory inhabited by people who retain ties to an older, more established parent state. The ties may be voluntary or forced.

Communism   political movement based on the writings of Karl Marx. Marx predicted that the working classes in industrial countries would revolt to create a workers' state in which a single political party would ensure fair shares for all, and eventually government itself would not be needed. In practice, Communist governments have often been dictatorships.

Communist   believer in Communism

confederation   loose grouping of states in which some may be more powerful than others

conscription   mandatory service in the armed forces

constitution   written document outlining the basic laws or principles by which a country is governed

devolution   passing some government powers of lawmaking and taxation to a lower-level body

dictatorship   government by a ruler (dictator) who has absolute power over the people he or she rules

dual citizenship   having the rights of a citizen in two states

duchy   territory ruled by a duke

exile   having to live outside a person's native country

Fascism   revolutionary political movement, beginning in Italy, that promised national glory in return for total obedience to a single political party headed by an inspired leader. Fascist governments tend to suppress free expression and political argument.

federation   grouping of states to achieve a common benefit, such as mutual defense or increased trade

Founding Fathers   common name for the leaders of the American movement for national independence from British colonial rule

guerrilla   soldier who fights in small-scale hit-and-run warfare; not a member of a regular army

idealistic   belief in such principles as duty, justice, and honor

imperialism   power or influence of one nation over others, as in an empire

military service   serving in a country's armed forces

Mughal   dynasty that claimed descent from the Mongols of Central Asia and ruled India from 1526 to 1857

multinational state   state inhabited by two or more nationalities

nationhood   status or identity of being a nation

nation-state   state inhabited by a single nation

native people people seen as indigenous, or belonging to, an area; for example, the Native Americans of the United States or the aboriginals of Australia

Orthodox belonging to the Orthodox Church, the main form of Christianity in Greece, Serbia, Russia, and neighboring countries

Ottoman Empire multinational empire of southeastern Europe and the Middle East, ruled by members of the Ottoman family until its collapse in 1920. The core area then became the Republic of Turkey.

Papal States territories in central Italy ruled by the Pope from 756 to 1870

parliament formal meeting to discuss public affairs. In some countries the name given to its legislative body.

patriotism love of one's country, people, and way of life

plebiscite vote of all the people of a country for or against a single proposal

political activist person who is very interested and involved in politics

post colonial state that has become independent from colonial rule

principality territory ruled by a prince

quinine medicine made from the bark of the cinchona tree and used to prevent or treat malaria. Quinine helped make the colonization of malaria-plagued parts of the world possible.

republic government headed by an elected president rather than a king or emperor born to be a ruler

republican in the manner, mode, or style of a republic. In the United States, Republican (with a capital R) is also used as the name of a political party.

royalist supporter of rule by kings

self-determination right of a group of people to govern themselves

separatist someone who wants to break away from an existing state

Socialist someone who has the political belief in the right of government to develop greater equality among citizens

sovereignty self-governing state

territory an area of land

Index

Dear Parents:

Congratulations! Your child is taking the first steps on an exciting journey. The destination? Independent reading!

STEP INTO READING® will help your child get there. The program offers five steps to reading success. Each step includes fun stories and colorful art or photographs. In addition to original fiction and books with favorite characters, there are Step into Reading Non-Fiction Readers, Phonics Readers and Boxed Sets, Sticker Readers, and Comic Readers—a complete literacy program with something to interest every child.

Learning to Read, Step by Step!

Ready to Read   Preschool–Kindergarten
• big type and easy words • rhyme and rhythm • picture clues
For children who know the alphabet and are eager to begin reading.

Reading with Help   Preschool–Grade 1
• basic vocabulary • short sentences • simple stories
For children who recognize familiar words and sound out new words with help.

Reading on Your Own   Grades 1–3
• engaging characters • easy-to-follow plots • popular topics
For children who are ready to read on their own.

Reading Paragraphs   Grades 2–3
• challenging vocabulary • short paragraphs • exciting stories
For newly independent readers who read simple sentences with confidence.

Ready for Chapters   Grades 2–4
• chapters • longer paragraphs • full-color art
For children who want to take the plunge into chapter books but still like colorful pictures.

STEP INTO READING® is designed to give every child a successful reading experience. The grade levels are only guides; children will progress through the steps at their own speed, developing confidence in their reading.

Remember, a lifetime love of reading starts with a single step!

Thomas the Tank Engine & Friends™

CREATED BY BRITT ALLCROFT

Based on The Railway Series by The Reverend W Awdry.
© 2015 Gullane (Thomas) LLC.
Thomas the Tank Engine & Friends and Thomas & Friends are trademarks of
Gullane (Thomas) Limited.
HIT and the HIT Entertainment logo are trademarks of HIT Entertainment Limited.
All rights reserved. Published in the United States by Random House Children's Books, a division
of Random House LLC, 1745 Broadway, New York, NY 10019, and in Canada by Random House
of Canada Limited, Toronto, Penguin Random House Companies.

Step into Reading, Random House, and the Random House colophon are registered trademarks of
Random House LLC.

Visit us on the Web!
StepIntoReading.com
randomhousekids.com
www.thomasandfriends.com

Educators and librarians, for a variety of teaching tools, visit us at RHTeachersLibrarians.com

ISBN 978-0-553-50747-8 (trade) — ISBN 978-0-375-97378-9 (lib. bdg.) —
ISBN 978-0-553-50748-5 (ebook)

Printed in the United States of America
10 9 8 7 6 5 4 3 2 1

THOMAS
& FRIENDS™

AS SEEN ON DVD!
DINOS
&
DISCOVERIES

THOMAS AND THE VOLCANO

Based on The Railway Series
by The Reverend W Awdry

Illustrated by Richard Courtney

Random House 🏠 New York

It was a busy day
on Sodor.
The Earl was building
a Dinosaur Park!

The park had models

of dinosaurs.

They were not real.

But they looked real!

Each engine had a job.
Thomas and Millie
carried trees and bushes
to plant.

Samson and Harvey
helped put the dinosaur
models together.

7

Suddenly, a dinosaur
head swung right
at Millie!

She screamed
and closed her eyes.
It stopped just in time!

Harvey and Samson
laughed at Millie.
"What a silly little
engine!" said Samson.

Millie was angry.
She tooted her whistle
and puffed away.

Millie wanted
to teach the big engines
a lesson.

But she and Thomas
had work to do!
They had to haul
wood for a bonfire.

Samson and Harvey
were working nearby.
They were building
a volcano.

"What is a volcano?"
asked Harvey.

"It is like a big firebox
filled with smoke
and lava!" Samson said.
Harvey was scared.

Millie heard
Harvey and Samson.
She had an idea.

"Build the bonfire

behind the volcano!"

she said to the workers.

Smoke rose into the sky.

Samson saw the smoke.

"The volcano is erupting!"

he cried.

Samson and Harvey
were scared!
They called for help
and sped away.
Millie's plan had worked!

Then the engines
heard Millie laugh.
"Silly big engines,"
she teased.
"It was just a trick!"

The Earl wanted
the tricks to stop.
The engines smiled
and agreed.

The engines kept
their promises.
They worked together.
They did not play
any more silly tricks.

The Earl was proud.
Soon the park was
ready for visitors.

What a team!